Pet Projects For Your Dog

PET PROJECTS FOR YOUR DOG

woof !

Mary-Anne Danaher

TIME
LIFE
BOOKS

CONTENTS

INTRODUCTION

Dogs should be rewarded for their unflinching loyalty, their excitement every time you walk through the door and their utter devotion. Not only is your dog your faithful friend, you are its best friend too! And best friends deserve to be spoiled sometimes.

Pet Projects for Your Dog is brimming with ideas for your beloved pooch, whether it yearns for a new kennel, dreams about gourmet foods or wishes for a little extra attention and quality time with you, there's something to suit all breeds, personalities and tastes.

The step-by-step photographs will have you making and finishing our easy projects in no time. With chapters on everything from making your dog's home a more beautiful and comfortable place to massage and bathing, travel tips and great ideas for indoor and outdoor play, *Pet Projects for Your Dog* is sure to become one of your (and your pooch's) favorite references.

Bring a little style, luxury and a sense of fun to your faithful friend's life with this inspirational book of ideas. All the projects in this book have been tried and tested by dogs and carry a resounding seal of approval. *Woof! Woof!*

bowls

jewelry

gifts

tasty treats

7

oui! oui!

AT HOME

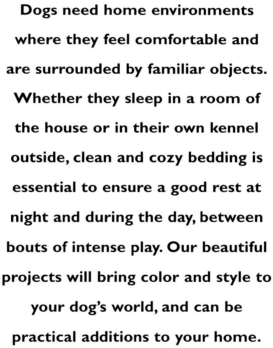

Dogs need home environments where they feel comfortable and are surrounded by familiar objects. Whether they sleep in a room of the house or in their own kennel outside, clean and cozy bedding is essential to ensure a good rest at night and during the day, between bouts of intense play. Our beautiful projects will bring color and style to your dog's world, and can be practical additions to your home.

HOME COMFORTS

Spoil your pet with our luxurious range of soft furnishings that are just perfect for lounging after a hectic day of play and activities. Your pet will love snuggling into our cozy quilt and cushion creations.

Appliquéd Bone Pillow

Materials: *20in (50cm) velour print fabric; sewing thread; 4in (10cm) red felt; embroidery thread; cushion insert or polyester toy filling.*

Cut two rectangles of fabric, 18in (45cm) x 24in (60cm). Place rectangles together, with right sides facing and stitch around all edges leaving a 6in (15cm) opening on one side.

Enlarge the bone template on page 78 to the desired size, trace and cut one bone from felt. Position bone in one corner of cushion and stitch in place, using embroidery thread, with blanket stitch (see page 79).

Place the cushion insert inside the cushion cover or fill it with polyester filling and stitch the opening closed.

Doggie Quilt

Materials: *20in (50cm) of each of two colors of washable mock suede fabric; 32in (80cm) contrasting colored washable mock suede or backing fabric; sewing thread; adhesive-backed felt in two colors; 20in (50cm) quilt batting.*

cozy pillow

1 Cut three 20in (50cm) x 5in (13cm) strips of each of the two main fabric colors. Stitch strips together lengthwise, alternating colors. Trim and neaten seams. Trace our paw prints from the Template and Patterns section on page 77 and transfer them to the paper backing behind the felt. Cut out these pieces and position as desired on the quilt top.

2 Pin and baste the quilt top piece to the batting and trim the batting to the correct size. With right sides facing, pin this piece to the backing fabric, stitching around all sides and leaving a 8in (20cm) opening. Trim seams and turn the quilt to the right side through the opening. Stitch the opening closed or use a row of clip fastenings to form the closure.

You may wish to stitch along the stripes, stitching through all layers to form a quilted effect. If doing so, ensure none of the felt paw prints overlap the seams.

stylish quilt

KENNEL CONVERSIONS

Your dog won't want to leave the privacy of its own stylish home after you've created one of these clever and quirky kennel makeovers. Follow one of our themes or create your own unique design.

Eiffel Tower Kennel

Materials: *Acrylic paints; paintbrushes; large cardboard box (approx 2 ¼ yards/2m long); pencil; craft knife; craft glue; acrylic varnish.*

Note: *This kennel is designed for a sheltered area and should only be placed outside in dry weather. To provide some weather resistance, seal the cardboard tower with one or two coats of sealer before painting it and apply four coats of varnish over the paint.*

1 Paint the kennel sides, front and roof with the desired colors. When dry paint French words or phrases (such as BONJOUR, AU REVOIR, CHIEN) on the kennel sides and allow to dry.

2 Cut a long piece of cardboard from the box and draw an Eiffel Tower outline in pencil. Copy the Eiffel Tower from a book or postcard. Cut out using a craft knife. Make sure to cut a front opening that corresponds with the kennel opening.

3 Cut supporting strips of cardboard and glue them in place behind the narrow sections of the tower. Paint the Eiffel Tower, and when dry, apply one or two coats of varnish.

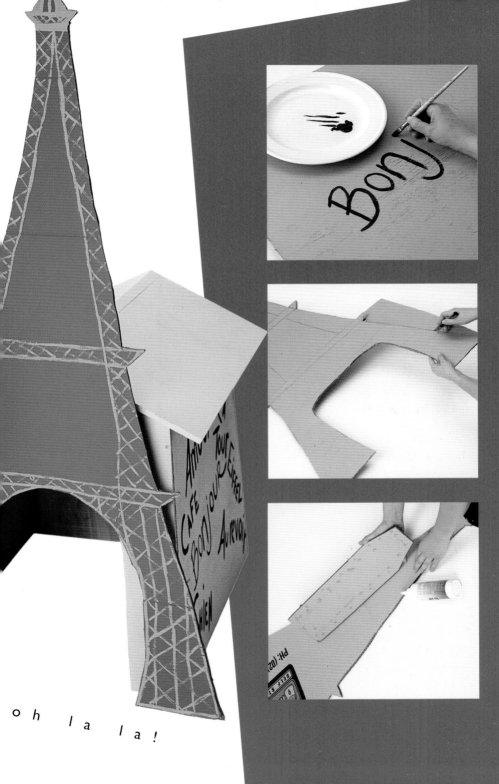

oh la la!

Glamour Chalet

Materials: *Metal shim (available at craft stores); craft knife or scissors; bath towel; tracing paper; blunt pencil; acrylic paints; craft knife; sealer; acrylic varnish; hot-glue gun and glue sticks.*

1 Cut strips of metal shim to fit around the sides and top of the kennel opening and along the center of the roof. Draw a flower motif (that is the correct size for the metal strips) on tracing paper, drawing three or four flowers in a row. Place a metal strip on a folded towel, place the tracing paper on top and trace over the design using the pencil. Draw freehand petals, swirls and other details between the flowers to create an elaborate design. Repeat for the other strips.

2 If placing the kennel outdoors, seal the metal strips on both sides with one or two coats of sealer (or use a rust-inhibiting product to paint it). Paint the kennel sides, front and roof the desired colors. Using hot glue, attach the metal strips to the front and roof of the kennel.

3 Paint other floral details around the kennel opening. When dry, apply one or two coats of varnish over the kennel and metal strips.

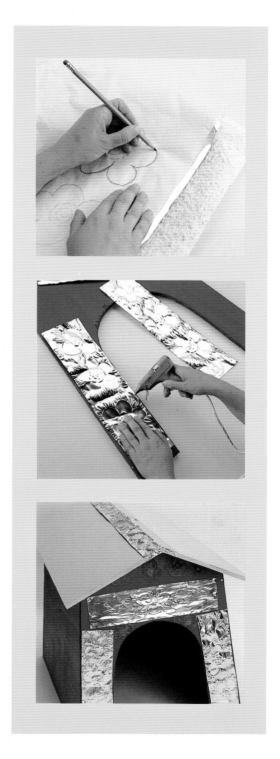

HOME ACCESSORIES

Create a colorful storage place for all your pooch's favorite toys so they can be neatly stored and are easy to find. Hang our subtly scented sachet inside your dog's kennel so everyone's nose knows the difference.

Scented Hanging Sachet

To make this doughnut-shaped sachet, cut two circles of gingham fabric with a 4in (10cm) diameter. Next, draw a 1½in (4cm) diameter circle in the center of each of these circles, using a water-soluble marking pen. Cut out this circle in both pieces of fabric to form a center hole in each piece.

Place the two pieces of fabric together, with right sides facing, and stitch around the inner and outer edges, leaving a 2in (5cm) opening in the outer circle. Turn the fabric sachet right side out through the opening.

Carefully fill the ring with dried lavender, then handstitch the opening closed. Attach a ribbon for hanging the sachet by looping it through the top of the sachet ring and stitching or gluing the ends of the ribbon together.

Paint the desired words on the front of the sachet using acrylic fabric paint. Stitch on other decorations such as ribbon roses.

When the fragrance fades, sprinkle a few drops of lavender oil on the surface of the sachet.

16

Toybox

Decorate a plastic crate with colorful cutout motifs to make a gorgeous and practical storage solution for your pet's toys. Use adhesive paper and trace the motifs onto paper (remembering to draw letters backward). Cut out the motifs and position them on the crate. Apply one or two coats of varnish over the surface of the crate to protect your design.

17

WHAT A DISH!

Personalize your dog's dinner bowl with a little paint and loads of imagination.

Felt-appliquéd Bowl

Draw, photocopy or print the required letters. You might like to spell out your dog's name, or words such as WOOF or DINNERTIME. Cut out the letters and trace them onto the paper backing on the felt, being careful to position the letters backward. Cut out, then stick the letters in place on the bowl. Add bone, heart or floral motifs to the end of the words to form a colorful decoration.

Painted Ceramic Bowl

Paint your own design, trace one that you like from a book or magazine, or use a stencil. Work the design on the outside of the bowl using a nontoxic air-drying ceramic paint or a nontoxic multipurpose acrylic paint that can be used on a range of different surfaces. Add motifs or words on the inside of the bowl and don't forget to decorate the rim with a simple pattern of spots, stripes or dashes or a mixture of these elements.

Stenciled Metal Bowl

Materials: *Pen; ruled stencil sheet; ruler; craft knife; acrylic paints; small sea sponge; fine paintbrush; acrylic varnish.*

1 Enlarge, trace and cut out the YUMMY stencil from page 78 and transfer it to a stencil sheet. You can use a ruled stencil sheet to make it easier to line up the letters. Working on a protected surface, cut out the stencil using a craft knife.

2 Position the stencil as desired on the bowl and lightly sponge over the letters using acrylic paint and a small sponge. For a modern look, try painting each letter separately to

form an interesting design, rather than a straight line. Paint other decorative details such as hearts, spots or dashes around the letters. When dry, paint a fine outline around the letters and motifs using a contrasting color, then apply one or two coats of varnish over the painted letters.

d i n n e r t i m e

19

THE FESTIVE SEASON FOR FIDO

Our beautiful Christmas projects will ensure your faithful friend feels part of the family festivities.

Christmas Stocking

This great stocking is made using our bone pattern on page 78. Enlarge and trace the design, then cut out two pieces of red felt using this pattern. Glue or stitch the pieces together around the edges and base, leaving the straight edge open. If stitching the pieces together, clip the seam around the curves, then turn it right side out.

Cut two strips of white fake fur fabric the width plus 1in (2.5cm) of the stocking top and about 10in (25cm) long. Place the strips with right sides facing and stitch together at the 10in/25cm edges, then turn right side out. Place this strip inside the stocking top with the fur side facing the inside of the stocking, align the edges at the stocking top and stitch along this seam. Trim excess fabric then turn the fur strip to the outside. Pin and stitch along the bottom edge of this strip, then attach a loop to hang the stocking.

ho! ho! ho!

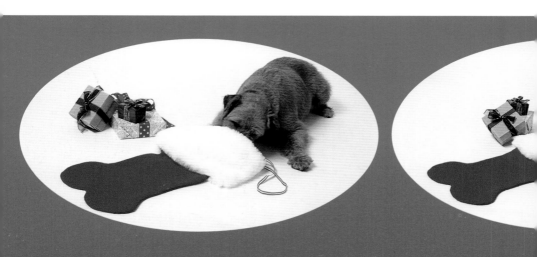

Doggie Advent Calendar

Materials: *Rectangular cardboard box; cardboard; glue; Christmas wrapping paper and cards; ruler; felt markers; craft knife; dog treats; ribbon; glue gun and glue sticks.*

1 Cut a piece of cardboard the same size as the top of the box and allow about ½in (12mm) extra all around. Make a Christmas collage design by gluing different colored and patterned pieces of paper and cards onto the cardboard. Rule lines to form boxes for the days from December 1 to 25 or the selected number of days and fill in the numbers. Decide which days are to have treats behind them and cut along three sides of these boxes to form doors.

2 Place this piece over the box and using a pencil, make marks on the inside of the box to indicate where to position the treats. Secure the treats in place using a little glue or restickable adhesive. Fold under the allowance around the edges of the collage piece and glue along these edges. Slip the collage piece inside the box so it sits flush with the top of the box. Decorate the outside of the box with ribbon, securing it to the top and sides of the box with hot glue.

Playtime

FOR PLAY

Dogs of all ages love to play and
our great toys and ideas for indoor
and outdoor activities will keep
them out of mischief. Puppies,
especially, will enjoy curling up with
our soft bear toy and will develop
their coordination skills when
playing with our cute jingle ball.
So stimulate your pooch by
introducing a new activity at the
park, and on rainy days, roll out our
interactive indoors playmat for
hours of fun inside the house.

THE GREAT OUTDOORS

Fit, healthy, fun-loving dogs will adore our easy-to-assemble agility course that's designed to give you and your pet many fun moments together. We've also included other ideas for activities that are designed to keep dogs out of mischief.

Chasing the stick and swimming

Try introducing your dog to water in summer, with a number of activities such as chasing a ball or stick. For dogs who need extra reassurance in the water, try wading out into the water with them for the first few times, until they discover their sea legs!! Swimming with another dog that is proficient in the water can also be a great inducement, as the two are likely to play and chase each other on the water's edge and splash through the shallows before swimming out into deeper water. Balls that float and are clearly visible on the surface are the best for your dog to chase. Some dogs though, will prefer to chase a stick and you can bring your own or find them at the park or beach. If you have more than one dog, use a long stick so they can bring it back to the shore together. By throwing the stick and asking them both to fetch it, they will both be getting great exercise. Running on the sand is also a good form of exercise for your dog, so throw your stick or ball and ask your dog to fetch it on land a few times before throwing it into the water. Digging in the sand is another fun activity. Show your dog the ball or stick, then dig a hole, throw it in and cover it with sand; tell your dog to find the object or dig for it.

splish splash

THE GREAT OUTDOORS

Portable Agility Course

Materials: *Four or six cardboard cylinders, approx. 2in (5cm) in diameter; two fanned garden stakes; strong tape; acrylic paint; nails, hammer; two cardboard boxes (one medium and one small).*

Whether you're interested in pursuing agility on a purely casual level or plan to work up to competition level, making your own jumps and other obstacles is the ideal way to begin. There are many dog agility clubs where dogs and owners learn to race against the clock while tackling challenging courses. If your dog has a lot of energy and requires plenty of exercise, then a homemade agility course will provide hours of entertainment. Set it up in your own backyard or take it to a local park or recreational area where dogs are allowed. Try to recycle pieces of wood, old tires and other objects from around your home, then use your imagination to assemble a range of interesting obstacles.

To make the jumps. Leaving the plastic lids on the ends of the cylinders, place two end-to-end and tape them together securely at this point. Repeat with the remaining cylinders to form other bars. Apply tape at intervals along one jump (this forms the top bar). Paint the cardboard between the tape and allow to dry.

Paint the remaining bars using two contrasting colors and apply paint on either side of the tape (these form the lower bars).

Paint the garden stakes, and on the back side of each stake, mark where the bars are to be positioned, ensuring the markings correspond on each stake. Hammer nails into the stakes at these points. Using the same size nails, mark small holes in the end of each bar so they will attach to the stakes. Assemble the stakes and bars outdoors. (You will need a hammer to push the stakes firmly into the ground.)

Other ideas for the agility course

Ramps These can be made from two pieces of sturdy board that are hinged together at the center and have a rope or chain suspended between them to prevent the ramp from flattening. You can also lean a sturdy board or plank up against a different level in a landscaped garden or park to allow your dog to climb the ramp then jump down from this height.

Tire trail Old tires can be placed close together to form a long course that your dog has to negotiate as it is running.

Tire hoop Suspend a tire with rope from a high branch of a tree and coax your dog to jump through it. You can also fix it to a wooden frame that is weighted at the base and will stand erect as your dog jumps through it.

Weave poles Attach a number of poles to a flat piece of wood so the poles stand upright about a dog's body width apart. You can also hammer single garden stakes into the ground, spacing them evenly to create the weave poles.

Collapsed tunnel Cut the base out of an old plastic pail then make holes around this edge and attach corresponding ties to secure an old bed sheet around the pail. Lay the pail on its side and secure it between two garden stakes so it does not move and roll when your dog crawls through it.

Walk the plank Place a wooden plank across two crates or wooden boxes. You may need to begin by using a wide plank, then as your dog's confidence grows, replace it with a narrower plank.

THE GREAT OUTDOORS

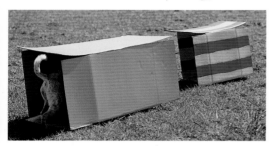

Tunnels

To make the tunnels, just paint the outside of two cardboard boxes, using the desired colors and allow to dry. You can paint the boxes using a single color or paint stripes using two contrasting colors. The boxes can be placed outdoors and to ensure they stay open and upright, fold in one or two of the flaps at one end of the box.

Bobbing for Balls in Water

Water play is always great fun and is best done outdoors or in an easy-to-clean area, as there are inevitably many spills involved with this activity. Lightweight plastic balls can be placed in a large container or basin of water, or try throwing the balls into the container and asking your dog to FETCH them as they float on the surface.

On a hot summer's day try substituting ice cubes for balls. Most dogs will enjoy fishing the ice out of the water then eating it to cool off. This is a very messy activity too, so set up the bowl in a laundry area or a covered outdoor area.

fetchin' fun

Catching the Ball and Running

Most dogs love balls and will chase them every time they are thrown. Some love to chase the ball and not give it up! If you persist with training when your dog's a pup you'll find that this game can be rewarding for both of you. Tell your dog to FETCH the ball when you throw it and then bring it HERE or DROP it. When your dog gets it right reward it with a pat or a treat.

To make your ball fly that extra mile, take a tennis racket to the park and serve up some great forehands for your pooch to chase. If your dog shows a lack of interest, try a few of the following alternatives, or perhaps it's just too tired to play any more.

🐾 Try hitting the ball underhand with the tennis racket so it flies up high into the air and allows your dog to become airborne when catching it.

🐾 Some dogs will prefer chasing sticks; you can pick these up on your walk to the park or at the park. When you've found a great stick take it home and bring it back to the park on every visit.

🐾 A frisbee is also a favorite with many dogs, as it maintains altitude and floats for longer, allowing your pooch to leap up and catch it in midair.

INDOOR ACTIVITIES

Our bright playmat is the perfect accessory for when it's too wet to venture out-of-doors. Artificial grass will never replace the real thing but dogs still love to crawl and roll on it! Attaching toys such as balls is a great way to provide extra entertainment for your pooch.

Indoor Grass Playmat

Materials: *1 yard (1m) synthetic grass; felt, in assorted colors; narrow elastic; tennis ball; glue gun and glue sticks; fabric binding tape; small piece fur fabric; adhesive felt letters.*

1 Tape the edges of the mat with a strong masking tape or similar tape. Overlap the ends of tape at the corners to create a firm and neat finish.

2 Cut a path and cloud shapes from felt and glue them in place on the mat. Cut a 1¼in (3cm) piece of fabric binding tape, fold it in half, and using hot glue, attach it by the raw edges onto the ball to form a loop. Cut a long piece of elastic and secure one end to the loop. Make a small hole in the mat and thread the other end of the elastic through to the back of the mat. Tie a double or triple knot so the elastic remains in place on the back of the mat.

TOYS

Our toys are sure to deliver hours of fun for your favorite pooch, and puppies will love curling up next to our comforting soft bear toy at night.

Fabric Bone

Make a bone-shaped cardboard template. Use it to cut two bone shapes from cotton fabric. Cut two 2in wide strips of the same fabric for the sides. Stitch these pieces together to form a bone cube, leaving a 2in (5cm) opening on one seam. Trim and neaten seams, clip curves and fill with polyester toy filling.

Cut the letters D, O and G from felt and using a contrasting colored thread, stitch these onto one side of the bone with running stitches.

Soft Bear Toy

Trace the bear toy template from the Templates and Patterns section on page 78 and enlarge it on a photocopier, if desired.

Cut two bear shapes from fake fur fabric. Place them together, right sides facing and stitch around all the edges leaving a 2in (5cm) opening on one side. Trim and neaten the seams.

Turn the bear right side out and fill with polyester toy filling, pushing the filling into the corners of the toy with a pencil or knitting needle. Handstitch the opening closed and tie a strip of ribbon or braid around the bear's neck.

bone toy

play time

TOYS

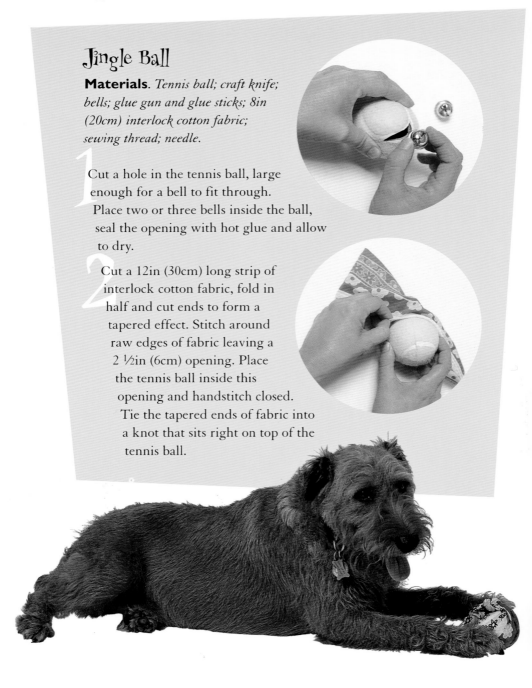

Jingle Ball

Materials. *Tennis ball; craft knife; bells; glue gun and glue sticks; 8in (20cm) interlock cotton fabric; sewing thread; needle.*

1 Cut a hole in the tennis ball, large enough for a bell to fit through. Place two or three bells inside the ball, seal the opening with hot glue and allow to dry.

2 Cut a 12in (30cm) long strip of interlock cotton fabric, fold in half and cut ends to form a tapered effect. Stitch around raw edges of fabric leaving a 2 ½in (6cm) opening. Place the tennis ball inside this opening and handstitch closed. Tie the tapered ends of fabric into a knot that sits right on top of the tennis ball.

bouncing
ball

jingle ball

woof! woof!

TO WEAR

Every dog deserves a makeover, whether it's just a fashionable new collar, a painted leash, a cozy knitted coat or a sassy vest to wear out on special occasions. Our range of gorgeous fashions and groovy collars are sure to please every pooch. There's even a backpack with plenty of pocket space for independent pooches that like to carry their own supplies on long walks.

HAUTE COUTURE

Dogs with fashion flair will love our colorful coats and collars and there's even a backpack for the intrepid walker.

Doggie Vest

Materials: *24in (60cm) cotton fabric; 12in (30cm) thin padding; fabric binding tape; sewing thread; 20in (50cm) webbed tape; 2 plastic buckle closures.*

1 Trace coat pattern from the Templates and Patterns section on page 76, place against your dog and enlarge or reduce on a photocopier, as desired. Cut two coat pieces from fabric and one from padding (if desired), place the padding between the two fabric pieces and pin and baste around all the edges.

2 Pin fabric binding tape around the edges, then stitch in place through all layers. Turn binding over edge to other side and handstitch in place with invisible stitches. Cut the desired length pieces of tape for the neck and chest closures. Thread tape through buckle pieces and pin neck pieces and chest pieces on coat to correspond. Try coat on your dog before stitching tape in place and adjusting, if necessary. Hand or machine stitch tape in position.

s a s s y
v e s t

Knitted Dog Coat

This simple-to-knit coat is worked in stocking stitch; knitting stitch embroidery decoration gives it a real tartan flair. Turn to page 74 for the knitting instructions.

k n i t t e d   c o a t

HAUTE COUTURE

Raincoat

Materials: *40in (1m) waterproof fabric or lightweight vinyl; sewing thread; 40in (1m) webbed tape; small piece fur, brushed cotton or interlock cotton fabric; glue gun and glue sticks; 20in (50cm) ribbon; 1 snap fastener.*

Trace the raincoat hood side and center pattern pieces from the Templates and Patterns section on page 76. Enlarge or reduce the pattern pieces on a photocopier so they fit your dog. Cut one rectangular piece of fabric large enough to fit your dog from the neck to the tail for the raincoat, two hood side and two hood center pieces.

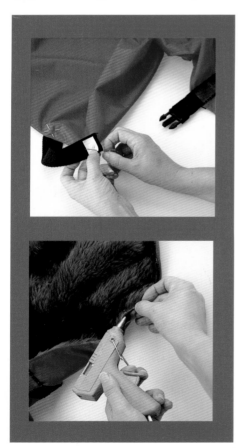

Fold under and stitch the raw edges around three sides of the raincoat piece. Gather the other edge. Stitch the two hood center pieces together and stitch a hood side piece to each outside edge of this piece. Fit the hood on your dog and adjust the seams, if necessary, then stitch, trim and neaten the seams.

With right sides facing, pin the straight edge of the hood to the gathered edge of the raincoat. Adjust the gathers to fit. Stitch, trim and neaten this seam.

Pin a length of webbed tape along this join on the inside and the outside of the raincoat and leave about 10in (25cm) of tape at one end and 4in (10cm) at the other end. Stitch through all layers.

Pin and stitch the clip end of the buckle to the shorter end of the tape and thread the buckle end onto the long end of the tape.

Cut another piece of tape about 5½in (15cm) long and stitch one end to the base hem of the raincoat. Stitch the corresponding pieces of a snap fastener to either end of this tape so when clipped together it forms a loop that fits around your dog's tail.

2 Trim the outside neck tape with a length of ribbon and glue it in place on the tape, using hot glue from a glue gun.

Cut a piece of fake fur, the same size as the inside of the hood, to form the lining.

Fold under and stitch around the raw edges, then pin it in place on the inside of the hood. Glue or stitch this fabric in place on the inside of the hood.

CAPTIVATING COLLARS AND JEWELRY

Every pooch will look their best when wearing one of our fabulous collars or personalized tags.

Jewel Collar

Decorate a plain leather collar with plastic jewels to create a stunning new look to wear. Using a hot-glue gun, secure plastic beads onto the surface of the collar, spacing and alternating them to create a great effect. Then the collar's ready to wear!

stunning

Stenciled Bone Collar

Materials. *Leather collar; stencil sheet; pencil; craft knife; cutting board; sealer; acrylic paints; stencil brush; fine paintbrush; varnish.*

1 Enlarge or reduce the bone pattern from the Templates and Patterns section on page 78 and transfer the design to the stencil paper. Working on a protected surface, carefully cut out the stencil using the craft knife, making sure you trim any uneven edges.

2 Apply a coat of sealer to the leather surface of the collar and allow to dry before painting. Work the bone design a number of times along the length of the collar, positioning it upright or sideways to create variation. Use two different paint colors, alternating them each time you paint the bone. Paint zigzag or straight lines between each bone motif. Allow to dry, then apply one or two coats of varnish and allow to dry.

43

CAPTIVATING COLLARS AND JEWELRY

Clay Tags

1 Break off small amounts of molding clay and warm between your hands until the clay is pliable. Repeat to make balls of each color. Working on a protected surface, press down on the balls to flatten them to the desired thickness. Using the pin, draw designs such as bones, flowers, hearts and diamonds in the clay, drawing them large enough to accommodate your dog's name, make smaller shapes for dog jewelry.

2 Roll out long lengths of two different colored clays, twist them together, then roll them to make a two-tone length. Use this to decorate the edge of tags or form into bow decorations. Make a hole in the top of each tag using a skewer. Place the shapes on a nonstick cookie sheet and bake, following the instructions on the package of clay. Remove from the oven and allow to cool, then attach rings to the tags so they can be hung from your dog's collar.

Materials. *Molding clay, in assorted colors; long sewing pin; craft knife; nonstick cookie sheet; skewer.*

TAKE ME WALKING

Going for a stroll or hike will be a great event with our stylish decorated leashes and a backpack that's designed for the adventurous hound.

Painted Leash

Create your own individual leash by working a painted design on a new purchase or transform an old leash into a fashion statement. Apply a coat of acrylic sealer to the leash and allow to dry before beginning to paint. Paint your own design along the length of the leash, repeat a pattern, paint a phrase such as "I Love My Owner" or "Best-Behaved Dog in the World" or combine colors to create an eye-catching design. When the paint is dry, apply one or two coats of varnish and allow to dry before taking your dog for a walk.

leash

lovely

Santa Fe Leash

Embroider a mesh leash with your own simple design, using tapestry wool in the desired colors and a tapestry needle. Our Santa Fe-influenced design features geometric lines worked in longstitch. A gold bead was stitched in the center of each pattern and repeated to complete the effect.

TAKE ME WALKING

Doggie Backpack

Materials: *20in (50cm) denim fabric; 12in (30cm) contrasting fabric; sewing thread; snap fasteners or Velcro; 12in (30cm) webbed tape; plastic carrier buckle.* (Use same template as dog coat but add pockets.)

get packing

1 Cut two pieces of denim fabric to fit around and down the length of your dog's body. With right sides facing, stitch these pieces of fabric together around three sides, leaving one long side open. (This becomes the top of the backpack).

Cut another strip of fabric, about 4in (10cm) x 2in (5cm), fold under

and stitch around all the edges of this piece. Fold the piece in half and pin it in position between the two layers of fabric to form a loop through which you can thread your dog's collar. Stitch along this top edge, stitching through all layers of fabric.

Cut two large pocket pieces to fit on each side of the main backpack piece and two pocket flaps to correspond. Fold under and stitch around all sides of these pieces. Pin the pockets and flaps in position on either side of the backpack. Try it on your dog. Before stitching the pockets in place, try it on your dog.

Cut strips of Velcro to fit along the pocket and pocket flap edges and form closures.

Thread your dog's collar through the loop at the top of the backpack and try the backpack on your dog to position the chest strap. Mark the position with a water-soluble marker or chalk and remove the backpack.

Cut the lengths of webbed tape required to fit your dog. Pin and stitch one piece of tape to one of the positions marked on the backpack. Loop the other piece through the plastic carrier, bring the ends together and pin and stitch them in place at the other mark on the backpack. The tape can now be threaded through the plastic carrier to secure the backpack in place on your dog's back.

Give your dog a break from the regular feeding routine by serving one of our delicious gourmet recipes. These healthy meals and snacks can become an integral part of your dog's diet or may be served as a treat on special occasions. If your dog is overweight, consult your vet for the best feeding and diet advice. Once you've begun to cook for your dog you'll find just how easy it is — and your faithful friend will reward you with loads of affection.

MEALTIME

yummy! yummy!

MAIN COURSE

Make your dog's main meal a wonderful treat every day with our selection of delicious recipes.

Kennel-loni

1lb (500g) ground chicken
1 teaspoon olive oil
1 tomato, diced
1 cup (8fl oz/250ml) chicken stock
5oz (155g) spinach, chopped
2 heaped tablespoons cottage cheese
canneloni

1 Heat oil in pan, add chicken and stir for 2 minutes. Add tomato, stock and spinach and simmer for 15 minutes.

2 Drain off excess liquid and reserve, then stir in cheese and fill canneloni tubes with mixture.

3 Place in baking tray, pour ½ cup (4fl oz/125ml) liquid on top and bake in a moderate oven (375–400°F or 190–200°C) for 20 minutes, turning during cooking and adding more liquid, if required.

4 Remove from oven and allow to cool until just warm. Serve topped with chopped tomato, if desired.

kennel-loni

Pooch Hotpot

1lb (500g) beef, cut into 1½in (4cm)
pieces
½ large onion, sliced
1 tablespoon olive oil
1 teaspoon tomato paste
2 cups/500ml beef stock
½ sweet pepper, sliced
3 large potatoes, chopped
2 bay leaves

1 Add all ingredients to pan. Bring to the boil then simmer, covered, over low heat for about 30 minutes until the liquid has halved. You may need to add water if the liquid evaporates too quickly.

2 Cool until just warm, then serve.

hotpot

Grr-Fry Chicken and Vegetables

6½oz (200g) chicken breast,
  chopped into cubes
1 large carrot, sliced
3oz (90g) green beans
½ sweet red pepper
fresh egg noodles
1 teaspoon soy sauce

1 Cook noodles following instructions on package and keep warm.

2 Heat wok, spray lightly with olive oil, add carrots, beans and pepper and stir-fry until they change color.

3 Remove vegetables from wok, add chicken pieces and stir-fry until they just change color.

4 Add vegetables and sauce and stir-fry lightly.

5 Cool until just warm, then serve.

s t i r - f r y

Tips

🐾 Don't overcook the meat in the recipes. Just allow it to change color. You may need to remove it from the pan during cooking our recipes, then add it just before serving.

🐾 These recipes can be served cold or just warm. The food should never be more than lukewarm. It should be cool enough for you to touch. Never overheat food or you may burn your dog's mouth. If using a microwave oven to heat food, heat it in small bursts until it reaches the desired temperature.

🐾 Add garnishes of raw vegetables such as carrots, beans and peppers when serving these recipes.

🐾 The recipes have been designed to make two servings but serve food as required according to your dog's size. If your dog is overweight, consult your vet before serving these recipes.

🐾 Introduce new foods slowly by adding a little more of a new food to each meal. You dog will soon begin to display its own taste and decide which recipes are to become special favorites.

🐾 Give treats sparingly. Use them as a reward when training your dog or serve them on special occasions. They will also be great additions to doggie party bags or Christmas stockings.

🐾 Serve our delicious meals in one of the decorated bowls from the At Home chapter on page 18 or paint plain white bowls and plates with quirky and colorful designs, as we have done. Oven-fired and air-dry china and ceramic paints are available from many craft stores.

MAIN COURSE

Woofy Pie

1lb (500g) lamb, cut into 1½in/4cm pieces
frozen pastry sheets
1 teaspoon olive oil
1 large carrot, chopped
3 large potatoes, chopped
3fl oz (100ml) beef stock
3oz (100g) frozen peas

1 Thaw pastry following instructions on package.

2 Heat pan over medium heat, add oil, then lamb and brown lightly. Remove lamb from pan.

3 Add remaining ingredients and simmer for 10 minutes, or until liquid has reduced and ingredients are just moist. Add lamb and stir gently.

4 Line base and sides of a lightly greased pie pan with pastry, fill with mixture and cover with another piece of pastry, sealing edges to form a pie.

5 Bake in a moderately hot (425–450°F, 220–230°C) oven for 20 to 30 minutes or until cooked.

6 Remove from oven and allow to cool until just warm, then slice pie and serve, adding a spoonful of cottage cheese, if desired.

sausage

Pupperoni Sausage

16oz (500g) ground beef
½ large onion, diced
1 large carrot, grated
1 egg, lightly whisked

1 Place all ingredients in a bowl and mix together to bind. Shape small amounts of mixture into sausages.

2 Heat pan and spray lightly with olive oil. Fry sausages until meat is just cooked.

3 Remove from pan, allow to cool until just warm and serve.

woofy pie

TASTY TREATS

Good dogs will love receiving these delectable treats in return for their excellent behavior or as a snack between meals.

Herb Basted Dog Biscuits

1 cup (5oz/150g) white flour
1 cup (5oz/150g) whole-wheat flour
⅓ cup (6 tablespoons) butter
1 egg, lightly beaten
4 tablespoons soy milk
2 tablespoons grated apple

Topping

½ cup cheddar cheese, grated
4 tablespoons parsley, finely chopped
4 tablespoons dried mixed herbs
1 egg, lightly beaten

1 Combine flours, butter, egg, milk and apple in a bowl and mix well. Form small amounts of dough into biscuit shapes, or roll out dough and cut shapes using cookie cutters.

2 Combine cheese, parsley and dried herbs in a bowl, mix well. Place beaten egg in another bowl. Dip each biscuit into the beaten egg then roll in dry mixture and place on a lightly greased baking tray. Repeat to make all the biscuits. Bake in a moderate oven (375–400°F, 190–200°C) for 20 to 30 minutes or until lightly browned.

Liver Biscotti

2 cups whole-wheat flour
3oz (90g) ground almonds
4 tablespoons dried liver or liver jerky
  (available at pet stores), chopped
6 tablespoons (90g) soft margarine
1 egg yolk
2 teaspoons water

1 Combine flour, almonds and liver in a bowl, rub in margarine, add egg yolk and water and mix to a firm dough.

2 Roll out dough thinly on a lightly floured surface and cut rounds or other shapes with cutters and place them on a lightly greased cookie sheet.

3 Bake in a moderate oven (375–400°F, 190–200°C) for 20 to 30 minutes or until lightly browned.

Bathtime need never be a drag for your dog with our simple step-by-step instructions for the perfect pampering session. As well as the basics of brushing and shampooing, we also teach you how to massage your dog into blissful contentment. There are also beautiful bathtime accessories to make for your dog or give away at birthdays and other festive occasions.

PERSONAL HYGIENE

bathtime

BATHING

Bathtime can be a ritual that every dog enjoys with our delightful accessories and easy steps for achieving bathtime bliss.

Fabric Appliquéd Towels

Make personalized bath towels for your faithful friend by trimming plain towels with strips of paw print or pooch motif fabric. Turn under the raw edges of the fabric, pin the strips in place along the woven bands of the towels and stitch them in place. This is also a great gift idea for pooch parties.

Bathing Rituals

Every dog needs a good washing every now and then, and if your dog spends a lot of time indoors, everyone's comfort will be increased by maintaining a regular bathing schedule.

Small dogs can be bathed in a sink, bathtub or even a laundry tub. Larger dogs, however, may need to be bathed outdoors using a garden hose and a bucket for rinsing. Wading pools can also be put to good use as bathtubs for larger animals.

Before bathing, remove your dog's collar and brush or comb the coat (see Brushing on page 60) to remove any tangles, burrs or other materials that have been caught in the coat.

1 When you have filled the bathtub with water at a suitable temperature lift your dog into the tub and soak the coat. Use a small bucket or an empty ice-cream container to pour water over your dog.

To avoid pouring water into your dog's ears, you may like to insert a small ball of cotton into the outer part of your dog's ear before bathing.

Apply the shampoo and work into a lather over your dog's coat. Start near the head or tail of your dog and work all over the body, massaging the shampoo right through the hair to the skin.

Clean around your dog's head and face using a damp cloth or sponge, then rinse off the shampoo. Remember to

remove all traces of
shampoo in your
dog's armpits and toes.

You may wish to repeat
or apply a conditioner.

2 When washing is finished, lift your
dog out of the tub and place on a
towel. Squeeze out the excess water
from your dog's coat with a second
towel. Rub your dog's coat following
the grain using fresh towels to
absorb the water. Use fresh towels as
needed.

When the towels are no longer
wet comb or brush your dog's coat to
ensure there are no tangles. Keep
your dog warm and away from dirt
while the coat is drying.

When the coat is completely dry brush
again to finish the grooming session.

GROOMING AND MASSAGE

Pampered pooches deserve the best in grooming and will love a massage to calm them down after a hard day at play.

Painted Grooming Set

Smarten up a plain brush and comb with a little acrylic paint. Paint a border, stripes, spots, hearts or dots or combine a number of these elements to create unique accessories. When the paint has dried, apply one or two coats of acrylic varnish to protect the painted surface.

Brushing

Brush your dog's hair to remove matted and tangled areas and dead hair cells. Brushing also helps the natural oils in your dog's coat permeate right through to the ends.

It takes very little time to brush your dog every day or every other day and in the long term this will promote a healthier coat and save you a lot of time trying the comb out nasty tangles.

Ask your vet's advice about which is the best brush for your dog's coat.

Massage

1 Begin to relax your dog with an all-over massage. Using cupped hands and sitting or kneeling behind your dog, drag your hand down on either side of the spine from the base of the neck to the tail. Work slowly and keep your hands level. Repeat this movement 10 or 20 times and feel your dog relax beneath your fingertips.

2 This technique is the perfect relaxer. Using your thumbs, place them on either side of your dog's head just near the ears. (You'll know the right spot as your dog will tell you and there are slight hollows just behind your dog's ears.) Work 40 to 60 circular motions on these spots using very light pressure in your thumb tips. Work in a clockwise direction first, then repeat in an counterclockwise direction.

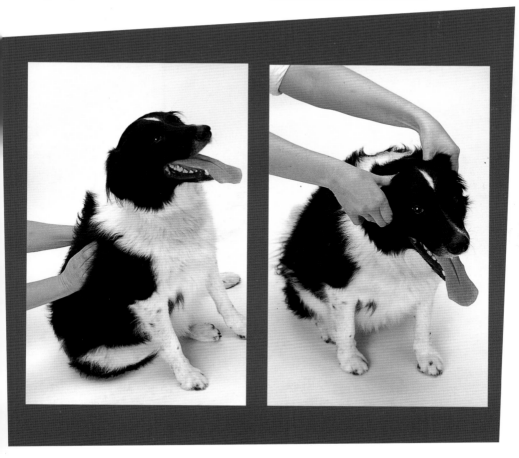

DOGGIE BAG

Chocky Bar

party time!

PARTY ANIMALS

Make every one of your dog's birthdays a landmark event with a doggie party. You may want to plan an intimate family affair or invite loads of friends to a lavish celebration. No matter what the size of the party, our ideas for making invitations and party bags, organizing great games and creating the birthday cake will ensure your party's a hit. We've also included a number of helpful tips to make certain everything runs smoothly on the big day.

PARTY ANIMALS

Dog parties can be a challenge, but a well-organized event will ensure that everyone goes home a little worn out, but happy!

Party Invitations

Make your own colorful party invitations from plain and corrugated colored cardboard. Cut out rectangular, square or unusual shapes for the cards.

Glue on pictures cut from magazines or bone and letter shapes cut from colored cardboard. Use paints and markers to write greetings on the outside of the cards and the important party details on the inside.

Healthy Canine Cake

1 ½ lb (750g) ground lamb
1 egg
1 cup oatmeal
½ cup almond meal
1 beef bouillion cube, crumbled
1 tablespoon cottage cheese
Low-fat cream cheese

1 Combine lamb, egg, oatmeal, almond meal, bouillion cube and cottage cheese in a bowl and mix well. Pour into a lightly greased cake pan or mold and cook in a moderate oven (375 C–400 F, 190–200 C) for about 1 hour or until cooked through.

2 Remove from oven and allow to sit for 5 minutes before turning onto a rack to cool. To create a bone-shaped cake, trace and enlarge our bone template from the Templates and Patterns section on page 78. Place the template on top of the cooled cake and cut around the outline with a sharp knife.

3 Decorate the cake with cream cheese or coat with pre-mixed sweet icing. Add sweet or savory treats and place a candle in the center.

happy birthday!

Doggie Bags

Brown paper bags make great doggie bags since they can be decorated using ink stamps, stickers, markers and colored pencils. Write the words "Doggie Bag" on the front of each bag, then decorate them accord-ingly with dog and bone shapes.

Fill them with dog biscuits, meat treats and caffeine-free dog chocolates.

Tie the bags up with ribbons and make sure every dog guest gets to take one home at the end of the party.

Games

Dog Biscuit Hunt. Ask a number of owners to hide bones in an area you have chosen for the hunt. (Remember to keep the dogs restrained or distracted while the bones are being placed.) Allow all the dogs to go and hunt for bones.

Some dogs are very possessive of their food so it's best to hold a game such as this on neutral territory and only if you are familiar with all the guests' personalities.

Doggie Paw-Print Mementos. Create charming plaster mementos for each guest to take home from the party. Just follow our instructions for the Walk of Fame tile on page 73 and each guest's paw print can be recorded for all time. Guests can take the tile home and ask their owners to paint it.

Party checklist and tips

🐾 Choose the guests and decide on the right balance of temperaments, personalities and sizes.

🐾 Select a suitable location (your backyard or favorite park). If it's raining, can you still have the party at this location or will you need to have a another plan?

🐾 Limit the party to one or two hours — this will give the dogs plenty of time to play without wearing out their owners.

🐾 When inviting dog friends it's always important to specify whether they should come on a leash and inform the owners about any rules at the park or location.

🐾 Make and send out the invitations.

🐾 Organize the games (see The Great Outdoors section of our For Play chapter on page 24 for ideas) and food and drink. Make sure there is enough food for the owners too.

🐾 Make the doggie bags.

Hope the weather is fine on the day!

c i a o !

BONE VOYAGE

Be prepared — our travel
accessories will ensure your dog
journeys safely, with all the
comforts of home close at hand.
Our cute doggie valise is large
enough to fit grooming essentials,
favorite toys and even treats to
keep your pooch occupied during
the journey and throughout the
vacation. Our cardboard car carrier
is designed to keep small and
medium dogs safely restrained on
long car trips.

BONE VOYAGE

Every dog on the move will love these essential travel items that make sure every journey's a safe and comfortable one.

Car Carrier

Materials: *Cardboard box; acrylic paints, in the desired colors; craft knife; strong tape or glue gun and glue sticks; small amount tulle fabric; holiday memorabilia such as airline luggage labels, postcards; ticket stubs, etc.*

1 Paint the carton and allow to dry. Cut an air vent about 8in (20cm) x 6in (15cm) in each end of the box, close to the base and bottom flaps. Assemble the box and tape or glue it together. Cut two pieces of tulle slightly larger all around than the vents, and glue them in place inside the box.

2 Decorate the outside of the box by gluing memorabilia in place and paint words onto the ends of the box, just above the vents. Make a long cut in each of the long top flaps of the box so the cuts correspond. When traveling, fold in the top flaps and secure by tying ribbon or rope through them. The carrier should be secured in a seat belt.

Doggie Valise

Materials: *Beauty case; 20in (50cm) dog print fabric; 40in (1m) ribbon; glue gun and glue sticks.*

1 Place the beauty case on top of the lining fabric and trace a light pencil line around the base onto the fabric. Cut out this piece and glue it inside base of the case.

2 Measure the distance around the case and cut a strip of fabric to fit, allowing a little extra so the ends can overlap. Fold under the raw edges of this strip and glue it in place around the case. Glue pieces of ribbon over the edges of this fabric strip to create a colorful contrast and a neat finish on the outside of the case. If desired, tie a ribbon bow around the case handle, so your pooch's luggage is easy to recognize.

Tips for Traveling

🐾 Make sure your dog wears a collar that records your home address and contact numbers. Your dog can also be fitted with a microchip, allowing him to be identified all over the country.

🐾 Try to feed and walk your dog at the same time every day.

🐾 When driving long distances, stop every couple of hours to rest and give your dog a bathroom and drink break.

🐾 Keep your dog on a leash when stopping by the roadside or in a park. There is no predicting what your dog will do in strange surroundings, so always err on the cautious side.

🐾 Pack some of your dog's favorite toys and treats and produce them during the journey.

🐾 Always restrain your dog in a car harness or in our car carrier, which can be secured with a seat belt.

🐾 If your dog is accompanying you on a flight, buy or rent a crate that is large enough for your dog. There are many companies that offer a crate rental service and door-to-door travel service for your dog. Place shredded newspaper in the bottom of the crate then place familiar objects, such as a small rug and toys, in the crate. These familiar smells will help calm your dog's nerves.

🐾 Speak with your vet for advice about sedating your dog.

Picture
Perfect

for me?

PRESENTS FOR DOG OWNERS

The ideal gift ideas for dog lovers —
our delightful range of handmade
gifts are easy to make and can be
personalized to include the
recipient's name, the dog's name,
and even a painted likeness of
the beloved pooch. We've even
included instructions for making
a tile that preserves your
pooch's paw print
for all time.

pooch print

PRESENTS FOR DOG OWNERS

Make these gorgeous gifts for friends and family members who just adore their dogs — or just for yourself.

Painted Dog Mug

Simply use paint to translate your ideas about your dog (or the recipient's dog) onto the surface of a coffee mug. Choose a nontoxic multi-purpose paint and varnish that can be applied to china and ceramics and doesn't require baking, then sketch your design on paper before transfering it to the mug.

You may like to include words such as WOOF, PUPPY LOVE, DOG or similar, a sketch of the dog or just colorful patterns in your design. Our design features simple colored blocks and text around the inside and outside rims of the mug. When the paint has dried, apply one or two coats of varnish over the painted surface of the mug.

Bone Picture Frame

Make a number of cute and colorful charms and letters from molding clay following our instructions for Clay Tags on page 44. Paint an old picture frame with a wash of your favorite color or purchase a new one. Use craft glue to attach the clay shapes and letters to the frame. Finally pick your favorite photograph of your dog and place it in the frame.

Walk of Fame Tile

Materials: *Air-dry molding clay (comes premixed in packet); bone biscuits or other shapes; acrylic paints; paintbrushes.*

1 Warm the clay between your hands then flatten it and form it into a square tile. Press a bone-shaped dog biscuit into the clay to form an impression and repeat this to form a border of bones around the outside edge of the tile.

2 Gently press your dog's paw into the center of the tile to form an impression, then allow the clay to harden according to the manufacturer's instructions. When dry, paint the bone and paw prints with acrylic paint, then paint the tile surface and allow to dry. Apply one or two coats of varnish over the entire tile, or if placing the tile outdoors, apply one or two coats of sealer before applying the varnish.

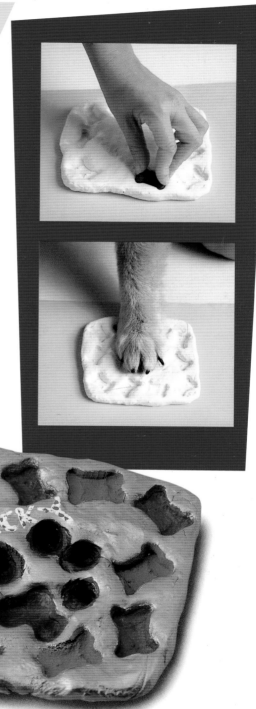

TEMPLATES and PATTERNS

TARTAN DOG COAT

Materials. 8ply knitting yarn (50g balls): Main Color (M — navy): 2 balls; 1st Contrast (C1 — gold): 2 balls; 2nd Contrast (C2 — red): ball. One pair each No.10 (3.25mm) and No.8 (4.00mm) knitting needles or sizes needed to give correct tension. Two stitch holders. One No. 8 (4.00mm) crochet hook for chain stitch.

Measurements (in/cm). To fit dog chest (in/cm): 18/45 (**22/55**, 26/65). Coat measures: 20/50 (**24/60**, 28/70). Center back length (incl neckband): 15/37.5 (**16½ /41**, 17½/44).

Tension. 22 sts and 30 rows to 10 cm over stocking st, using No.8 (4.00mm) needles. Please check your tension carefully before commencing. Wrong tension will result in a coat that is the wrong shape or size.

Abbreviations: alt: alternate; **beg:** beginning; **cm:** centimeters; **dec:** decrease; **rem:** remain; **rep:** repeat; **st/s:** stitch/es; **stocking st:** 1 row knit, 1 row purl.

BACK

Using No.10 (3.25mm) needles and M, cast on 57 (**67**, 77) sts.

1st row. K2, * P1, K1, rep from * to last st, K1.

2nd row. K1, * P1, K1, rep from * to end.

Rep 1st and 2nd rows 3 times more ... 8 rows rib in all.

Change to No. 8 (4.00mm) needles. ******

Work in stocking st stripes of 4 rows C2, 2 rows C1, 4 rows C2, 4 rows M, 2 rows C1, and 4 rows M until work measures 14/35 (**15/38**, 16½/41) cm from beg, ending with a purl row. Leave sts on a stitch holder.

BACK SIDE EDGINGS

With right side facing, using No. 10 (3.25mm) needles and M, knit up 97 (**107**, 117) sts evenly along one side edge of back, incl lower band.

Work 7 rows rib as for Back, beg with a 2nd row.

Cast off loosely in rib.

Work same edging along other side of Back.

FRONT

Work as for Back to ******.

Using C1 for rem, work 16 rows stocking st.

Shape for front legs. Cast off 7 sts at beg of next 2 rows ... *43 (53, 63) sts*.

Dec at each end of next and alt rows until 29 (**35**, 41) sts rem.

Work 31 rows stocking st.

Leave sts on stitch holder.

FRONT LEG EDGINGS

With right side facing, using No.10 (3.25mm) needles and M, knit up 44

(**48**, 52) sts evenly along one side of front leg shaping.

Knit 3 rows garter st.

Cast off loosely knitways.

Work same edging along other side of front leg shaping.

NECKBAND

With right side facing, using No. 10 (3.25mm) needles and M, knit across sts from front stitchholder, knit up 5 sts across Back Side Edging, knit across sts from back stitch holder, then knit up 6 sts across other Back Side Edging ... *97 (113, 129) sts*.

Work 11 rows rib as for back, beg with a 2nd row.

Cast off loosely in rib.

TO MAKE UP

With a slightly damp cloth and warm iron, press lightly on wrong side. Tie a colored thread in center st of Back (in first row of stocking st), miss 6 sts either side of center st and tie a colored thread in next st on either side, cont tying colored threads in every 7th st from previous colored thread to side edges.

With right side facing, using No. 8 (4.00mm) hook and C1, work row of Vertical Chain Stitch in center of stitch either side of marked sts, beg at first row of stocking st and working each chain st over 2 rows. Darn in all ends on wrong side. Using back stitch, join neckband seam. Slip stitch top ends of Front Side Edgings underneath Back Side Edgings at neckband. Slip stitch side edges of front to side edges of Back (on wrong side) at knit up row of Back Side Edgings, placing cast-on edge of Front 4 ¾/11 (**5/13**, 6/15) up from cast-on edge of Back.

VERTICAL CHAIN STITCH

Holding yarn at back of work and using crochet hook, draw a loop through to right side of work. Insert hook through stitch 2 rows above and draw another loop through, then through loop on hook. Continue in this manner, noting that yarn is carried at back of work and taking care not to pull sts too tight.

Tartan dog coat designed by Lucia R. Design

TEMPLATES and PATTERNS

Enlarge or reduce patterns,
using a photocopier to
achieve the appropriate size
for your dog.

Doggie Waistcoat pattern

See page 38 for photo
and instructions.

Raincoat hood side piece

See page 40 for photo and instructi

Paw prints for Doggie Quilt

See page 10 for photo
and instructions.

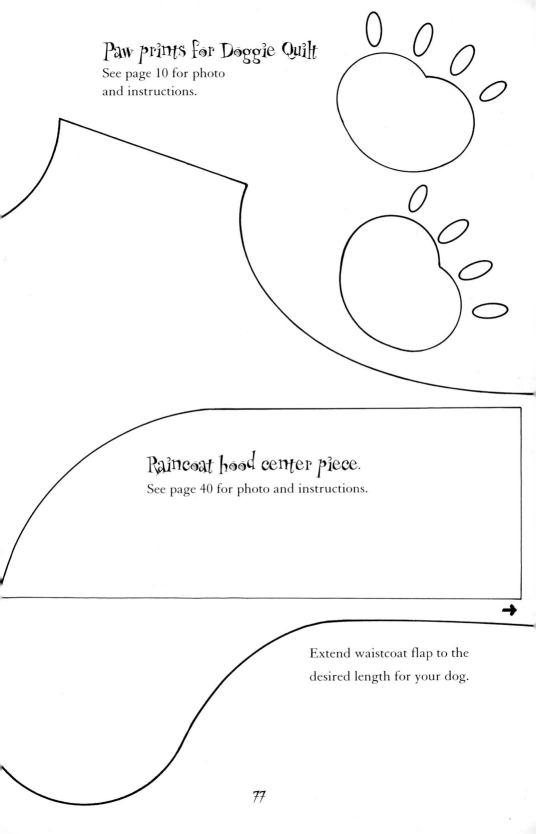

Raincoat hood center piece.

See page 40 for photo and instructions.

Extend waistcoat flap to the

desired length for your dog.

TEMPLATES and PATTERNS

Extend by 10in (25cm)

Enlarge or reduce patterns, using a photocopier to achieve the appropriate size for your dog.

Soft Bear Toy

See page 32 for photo and instructions.

letters for Stenciled Dog Bowl

YUMMY

See page 19 for photo and instructions.

Bone Stocking

See page 20 for photo
and instructions.

Bone for Appliquéd Bone
Pillow on page 10, Felt-
Appliquéd Bowl on page 18,
Stenciled Bone Collar on
page 43.

See page 19 for photo
and instructions.

BLANKET STITCH

Time Life Books is a division of Time Life Inc.
TIME LIFE INC. U.S.A.
President and CEO: George Artandi
Executive Vice President: Lawrence J. Marmon

Time-Life CUSTOM PUBLISHING
Vice President and Publisher   Neil Levin
Director of Acquisitions and Editorial Resources   Jennifer Pearce
Editor   Linda Bellamy
Director of Creative Services   Laura McNeill
Technical Specialist   Monika Lynde

Produced by Lansdowne Publishing Pty Ltd
©1999 Lansdowne Publishing Pty Ltd
First published 1999

Library of Congress Cataloging in Publication Data
Danaher, Mary-Anne.
    Pet Projects for your dog:easy ways to pamper your puppy/by Mary-Anne
    Danaher
    p. cm.
Includes index.
ISBN 0-7370-0054-6 (softcover: alk.paper)
1. Dogs--Equipment and supplies. 2. Handicraft. 3. Gifts.
I. Title
SF427.15.D25 1999   99-29321
636.7'0028'4--dc21   CIP

Printed in Hong Kong

Books produced by Time-Life Custom Publishing are available at a special bulk
discount for promotional and premium use. Custom adaptations can also be created
to meet your specific marketing goals. Call 1-800-323-5255.